Praise f
Power from On High

"Bishop McCaig addresses with insight the challenges and opportunities of embracing one's charisms. I recommend it highly to all who wish to understand or deepen their experience of God's gifts."

—**Terrence Prendergast, SJ, Emeritus Archbishop of Ottawa-Cornwall**

"Bishop Scott McCaig has crafted a short well-researched introduction to the Church's teaching about charisms, their missional purpose, and their powerful impact upon individuals, the Church as a whole, and the growth of the kingdom of God. Bishop McCaig addresses crucial issues: the relationship of the charismatic and hierarchical dimensions of the Church, charisms and discipleship, and the roles of the hierarchy and individual Christians in the essential task of discerning charisms. *Clothed with Power from On High* is a unique background resource for clerical and lay leaders who are looking for a quick solid introduction to the theology of charisms."

—**Sherry Weddell, Co-Founder and Executive Director of the Catherine of Siena Institute**

"In this short catechesis, Bishop Scott has collected and synthe-sized the rich teaching of Scripture, the early Church Fathers, the Magisterium, the saints, and recent popes on the critically important but often misunderstood role that charisms are meant to play in the life of the Church. For anyone, whether clergy or laity, who is looking to lay hold of the Church's fun-damental teaching and pastoral understanding of the exercise of charisms, this short book is a good place to start."
—Peter Herbeck, Vice President and Director of Missions, Renewal Ministries

"The whole Church needs more openness to the power and workings of the Holy Spirit. Bishop Scott McCaig's book is an important contribution to preparing a way for this to hap-pen. In a relatively short but comprehensive "catechism," this book answers the questions that many people have about the meaning and exercise of charisms. May many benefit from its research and wisdom!"
—Ralph Martin, STD, Director of Graduate Theology Programs in the New Evangelization, Sacred Heart Major Seminary, Archdiocese of Detroit

"If you want to experience your faith less like a syllogism and more like a love affair, read this short book on the charisms. God is on the move, and he's inviting us to be part of some-thing dangerous and beautiful."
—Matt Fradd, Catholic apologist and host of Pints with Aquinas

Clothed *with* Power *from* On High

A Short Catechesis on Charisms in the Life and Mission of the Church

Bishop Scott McCaig, CC
Foreword by Dr. Mary Healy

Copyright © 2023 Scott McCaig
All rights reserved.
Published by The Word Among Us Press
7115 Guilford Drive, Suite 100
Frederick, Maryland 21704
wau.org

27 26 25 24 23   1 2 3 4 5

ISBN: 978-1-59325- 713-2
eISBN: 978-1-59325-714-9

Design by Suzanne Earl

Library of Congress Control Number: 2023906958

To Fr. Bob Bedard, CC, my spiritual father in Christ, for revealing so authentically the unconditional love of God the Father and the wonderful adventure of living as a disciple of Jesus in the dynamic power of the Holy Spirit. Thank you.

Laeti bibamus sobriam profusionem Spiritus.
(Let us joyfully taste the sober intoxication of the Spirit.)
—St. Ambrose

Contents

Foreword

Dr. Mary Healy

Sixteen hundred years ago, St. Augustine, bishop of Hippo in North Africa, subscribed to the view that the supernatural gifts of the Spirit had all but disappeared from the life of the Church. He considered that although such signs of God's power had been needed for the initial growth of the Church, by his time they had long since ceased. The miracles done in the age of the apostles, he wrote, "were not permitted to last till our times, lest the mind should always seek visible things, and the human race should grow cold."[1]

Years later, Augustine was happily forced to change his mind. In one of his later and best-known books, *City of God*, he wrote, "Even now, therefore, miracles are wrought, the same God who wrought those we read of still performing them, by whom he will and as he will."[2] He goes on to recount numerous extraordinary works of God with which he was personally familiar, including healings from blindness, hemorrhoids, cancer, gout, paralysis, hernia, vehicle injuries, and demon possession, as well as prophetic dreams, miraculous financial provision, and even raisings of the dead.

On his very deathbed, the saintly bishop was granted yet another proof of the presence and activity of the Holy Spirit. As Augustine's friend Possidius, bishop of Calama, recounts,

When he was sick and confined to his bed there came a certain man with a sick relative and asked him to lay his hand upon him that he might be healed. But Augustine answered that if he had any power in such things he would surely have applied it to himself first of all; to which the stranger replied that he had had a vision and that in his dream these words had been addressed to him: "Go to the bishop Augustine that he may lay his hand upon him, and he shall be whole." Now when Augustine heard this he did not delay to do it, and immediately God caused the sick man to depart from him healed.[3]

By the grace of God, something like Augustine's renewed expectation of the manifest power of the Holy Spirit is happening in our own time. In our age of growing hostility to faith, of deepening moral and spiritual darkness, the Lord has been once again lavishing supernatural charisms on his people, in a profusion and variety perhaps not seen since the age of the apostles. Gifts of healing, prophecy, dreams and visions, and even miracles, alongside more "ordinary" charisms like teaching, service, and administration, are becoming more common. These gifts are the full equipment given by the risen Lord to his bride, the Church, empowering her to carry out her daunting mission to proclaim the gospel in power to a wounded and weary world.

It is natural for some Catholics and other Christians to have some skepticism about the charisms, as Augustine once did. Sometimes the gifts are associated with sensationalism and emotionalism. Sometimes they have been used in an immature, insensitive way that has given offense to others. There are charlatans whose supposed healings were later discovered to be staged. Even where the Holy Spirit's gifts are genuine, it is not easy to know how to discern them and how to pastor them wisely.

This is why Bishop Scott McCaig's book is such a timely and needed resource. It is written by a bishop and pastor of souls, in language that speaks to other pastors but also to laypeople thirsty to know more about the gifts of the Spirit. Bishop McCaig explains why the hierarchical and charismatic dimensions of the Church are not opposed to each other, but complementary, like the banks of a river and the rushing water that flows between them. He demonstrates that the Holy Spirit gives charisms to all, and that extraordinary charisms are not to be feared but are extraordinarily effective for building up the Church.

Jesus Christ did not die and rise from the dead for a powerless Church, unable to cope with the cynicism, brokenness, and spiritual emptiness that surround us. He died and rose to form a people alive in him, filled with joy, walking in the gifts and power of the Holy Spirit, bearing witness to his victory over sin and death! May this book be a source of encouragement to all who read it to take a brave step, enter into the flowing torrent of the Holy Spirit, and discover those marvelous gifts by which we have been "clothed with power from on high" (Luke 24:49).

Introduction

The divine mystery of the relationship between the Holy Spirit and the Church is beautifully and penetratingly summarized in the *Catechism of the Catholic Church*: "The Church is the Temple of the Holy Spirit. The Spirit is the soul, as it were, of the Mystical Body, the source of its life, of its unity in diversity, and of the riches of its gifts and charisms" (809).

One of these wonderful and diverse actions of the Holy Spirit is that of distributing charisms among the people of God. Charisms are tremendously important in the life and mission of the Church, though they have been more evident and recognizable at certain times in Church history. At a time when a fresh wave of charisms was appearing throughout the world, Pope St. Paul VI powerfully confirmed their importance:

> The Lord wishes to make the Church richer, more animated, and more capable of defining herself, of documenting herself, and this is precisely called "the effusion of charisms." Today much is said about it. Having taken into account the complexity and delicateness of the subject, we cannot but desire that these gifts come—and may God grant it—with abundance.[4]

It is an unfortunate reality, however, that many well-intentioned and sincere Christians simply do not understand why the charisms matter. For others, there are serious misunderstandings or points of confusion about the presence and role of charisms in the life of Christ's disciples. As we carefully consider what the Church actually teaches about the rich variety of charisms, we will also encounter the reasons why they are so important and answer these sincere questions and objections. In the full light of the teaching of the Church, we find that these obstacles begin to evaporate.

This subject is neither trivial nor of merely academic concern. We need to understand charisms because they are important in the life and mission of the Church. They are the action of the Holy Spirit, who is the very soul of the Church, and they are part of God's plan for the whole Church and for each and every Christian. They manifest God's providence, his specific call to each of us as individuals, and his passionate, all-embracing love for the whole world. They are the means by which we are "clothed with power from on high" (Luke 24:49) in order to fulfill the great commission of Jesus who told us, "Go therefore, and make disciples of all nations, baptizing them in the name of the Father, and of the Son, and of the Holy Spirit, teaching them to observe all that I have commanded you" (Matthew 28:19-20).

In order to see this more clearly, we will explore the rich bounty of the Sacred Scriptures. Then we will seek to break open and understand Scripture more fully by looking at the teaching of the Church Fathers, the Second Vatican Council, the *Catechism of the Catholic Church*, the consistent teaching of recent popes, and the theological insight of distinguished theologians. In a short catechesis such as this, I cannot cover all aspects of the topic, but I hope to give a solid understanding of the important place charisms have in the life and ministry of the Church.

CHAPTER ONE

What Is the Official Teaching of the Catholic Church about Charisms?

The Second Vatican Council clearly enunciated the Church's faith regarding charisms of the Holy Spirit:

It is not only through the sacraments and the ministries of the Church that the Holy Spirit sanctifies and leads the people of God and enriches it with virtues, but, "allotting his gifts to everyone according as He wills (1 Cor. 12:11), He distributes special graces among the faithful of every rank. By these gifts He makes them fit and ready to undertake various tasks and offices which contribute toward the renewal and building up of the Church, according to the words of the Apostle: "The manifestation of the Spirit is given to everyone for profit" (1 Cor. 12:7). These charisms, whether they be the more outstanding or the more simple and widely diffused, are to be received with thanksgiving and consolation, for they are perfectly suited to and useful for the needs of the Church.[5]

What Is a Charism?

The Sacred Scriptures tell us a great deal about charisms. We find the New Testament's teaching on charisms primarily in the letters of St. Paul, but also in the first letter of St. Peter, as well as in many other passages that refer indirectly to charisms. Although the Greek word *charisma* has the general meaning of "gratuitous gift," in the Scriptures the word has a very particular meaning. In Scripture, charisms refer to specific gifts that the Spirit distributes to individuals (see 1 Corinthians 12:10).[6]

Charisms are far more than human abilities. They are "the manifold grace of God" (1 Peter 4:10, NRSVCE), and each charism "is what might be called a 'gracelet,' a droplet of the vast ocean of God's grace."[7] The Scriptures are clear that they have a divine origin: charisms are "manifestation[s] of the Spirit" (1 Corinthians 12:7; see 1 Corinthians 12:4-11); are apportioned by the risen and ascended Christ Jesus (see Ephesians 4:7); and come to us from God (see Romans 12:3; 1 Corinthians 12:28; 2 Timothy 1:6). They are supernatural gifts lavished on us by the divine Persons of the Holy Trinity.[8]

As noted by prominent theologians, charisms have important spiritual characteristics. To begin with, charisms do not flow from sanctifying grace (which is infused into the soul at Baptism), and as a result, they are unique. God gives them completely gratuitously—we cannot merit them. This means that growth in holiness does not produce them or demand them.[9] Second, in every instance they require the direct intervention of God.[10] The New Testament identifies them as spiritual gifts (*pneumatika*), and this underscores that they "are bestowed by the Spirit (*pneuma*) and require a yielding to the influence of the Spirit."[11] Third, the state of grace is not required for the reception or exercise of a charism. One may be in a state of mortal sin and still exercise a charism. Although it is generally considered rare and by way of exception, it is even possible to manifest a charism before one is baptized (see Acts 10:44-48).[12]

It is evident, then, that the mere presence of a charism in a person's life says nothing about the state of their soul or about their personal holiness.[13] It is also true, however, that the proper exercise of a charism is itself an act of love that sanctifies the person who exercises it.[14] Finally, charisms are not necessary for the salvation of an individual.[15] However, as we shall see, they may be decisive for the salvation of others.

Charisms are not ends in themselves. They serve the loving will of God. It is easy to see why, as St. Paul insists,

> If I speak in the tongues of men and of angels, but have not love, I am a noisy gong or a clanging cymbal. And if I have prophetic powers, and understand all mysteries and all knowledge, and if I have all faith, so as to remove mountains, but have not love, I am nothing. If I give away all I have, and if I deliver up my body to be burned, but have not love, I gain nothing. (1 Corinthians. 13:1-3)

Jesus himself warned,

> "Not everyone who says to me, 'Lord, Lord,' will enter the kingdom of heaven, but the one who does the will of my Father who is in heaven. On that day many will say to me, 'Lord, Lord, did we not prophesy in your name, and cast out demons in your name, and do many mighty works in your name?' And then will I declare to them, 'I never knew you; depart from me, you workers of lawlessness.'" (Matthew 7:21-23)

It is critical to understand that charisms only make sense—and only have benefit for someone—if they are integrated into a life immersed in God's love through prayer, sacraments, and good works,[16] "a life transfigured by God's presence."[17]

What Are the Various Charisms We Can Receive?

Sacred Scripture mentions an array of these special charisms, including the following:

> For as in one body we have many members, and the members do not all have the same function, so we, though many, are one body in Christ, and individually members one of another. Having gifts that differ according to the grace given to us, let us use them: if prophecy, in proportion to our faith; if service, in our serving; the one who teaches, in his teaching; the one who exhorts, in his exhortation; the one who contributes, in generosity; the one who leads, with zeal; the one who does acts of mercy, with cheerfulness. (Romans 12:4-8)

> Now concerning spiritual gifts, brothers, I do not want you to be uninformed. . . .
> Now there are varieties of gifts, but the same Spirit; and there are varieties of service, but the same Lord; and there are varieties of activities, but it is the same God who empowers them all in everyone. To each is given the manifestation of the Spirit for the common good. For to one is given through the Spirit the utterance of wisdom, and to another the utterance of knowledge according to the same Spirit, to another faith by the same Spirit, to another gifts of healing by the one Spirit, to another the working of miracles, to another prophecy, to another the ability to distinguish between spirits, to another various kinds of tongues, to another the interpretation of tongues. All these are empowered by one and the same Spirit, who apportions to each one individually as he wills. (1 Corinthians 12:1, 4-11)

> Now you are the body of Christ and individually members of it. And God has appointed in the church first apostles, second prophets, third teachers, then miracles, then gifts of healing, helping, administrating,

and various kinds of tongues. Are all apostles? Are all prophets? Are all teachers? Do all work miracles? Do all possess gifts of healing? Do all speak with tongues? Do all interpret? But earnestly desire the higher gifts. (1 Corinthians 12:27-31)

Pursue love, and earnestly desire the spiritual gifts, especially that you may prophesy. For one who speaks in a tongue speaks not to men but to God; for no one understands him, but he utters mysteries in the Spirit. On the other hand, the one who prophesies speaks to people for their upbuilding and encouragement and consolation. (1 Corinthians 14:1-3)

When you come together, each one has a hymn, a lesson, a revelation, a tongue, or an interpretation. Let all things be done for building up. (1 Corinthians 14:26)

But grace was given to each one of us according to the measure of Christ's gift. Therefore it says:

> "When he ascended on high he led a host of captives,
> and he gave gifts to men." . . .

And he gave the apostles, the prophets, the evangelists, the shepherds and teachers, to equip the saints for the work of ministry, for building up the body of Christ. (Ephesians 4:7-8, 11-12)

God also bore witness by signs and wonders and various miracles and by gifts of the Holy Spirit distributed according to his will. (Hebrews 2:4)

Above all, keep loving one another earnestly, since love covers a multitude of sins. Show hospitality to one another without grumbling. As each has received a gift, use it to serve one another, as good stewards of God's varied grace: whoever speaks, as one who speaks oracles of God; whoever serves, as one who serves by the strength that God supplies—in order that in everything God may be glorified through Jesus Christ. To him belong glory and dominion forever and ever. Amen. (1 Peter 4:8-11)

Then Moses said to the people of Israel, "See, the LORD has called by name Bezalel the son of Uri, son of Hur, of the tribe of Judah; and he has filled him with the Spirit of God, with skill, with intelligence, with knowledge, and with all craftsmanship, to devise artistic designs, to work in gold and silver and bronze, in cutting stones for setting, and in carving wood, for work in every skilled craft. And he has inspired him to teach, both him and Oholiab the son of Ahisamach of the tribe of Dan. He has filled them with skill to do every sort of work done by an engraver or by a designer or by an embroiderer in blue and purple and scarlet yarns and fine twined linen, or by a weaver—by any sort of workman or skilled designer." (Exodus 35:30-35)

The disciples said to him, "If such is the case of a man with his wife, it is better not to marry." But he said to them, "Not everyone can receive this saying, but only those to whom it is given. For there are eunuchs who have been so from birth, and there are eunuchs who have been made eunuchs by men, and there are eunuchs who have made themselves eunuchs for the sake of the kingdom of heaven. Let the one who is able to receive this receive it." (Matthew 19:10-12)

I wish that all were as I myself am [celibate]. But each has his own gift from God, one of one kind and one of another. (1 Corinthians 7:7)

Jesus said to him, "If you would be perfect, go, sell what you possess and give to the poor, and you will have treasure in heaven; and come, follow me." (Matthew 19:21)

"And these signs will accompany those who believe: in my name they will cast out demons; they will speak in new tongues; they will pick up serpents with their hands; and if they drink any deadly poison, it will not hurt them; they will lay their hands on the sick, and they will recover." (Mark 16:17-18)

Most scriptural references to charisms are from the New Testament because "although the phenomenon, if not the name, of charismatic gifts was evident in the Old Testament (e.g., in Moses, the Prophets), the full outpouring of the Spirit was reserved for messianic times (Ps 67:19; Eph 4.7–13)."[18] It is also important to note that "none of these lists claims to be exhaustive."[19] The range of diversity of these special gifts allotted by the Holy Spirit may be immense. In fact, St. Irenaeus explains that it is impossible to number the charisms.[20] One obvious example is the charism of infallibility in matters of faith and morals, which is given, under certain conditions, to the Church's shepherds (see *Catechism*, 890–892).

It is important to note that while a few of the gifts are of an extraordinary nature, such as healing, deliverance, or prophecy, most charisms are seemingly very ordinary, such as hospitality, administration, or teaching. In God's economy, each charism has its own place and importance.

Who Can Receive Charisms?

It is a common misconception that only a few extraordinary souls can receive supernatural gifts from the Holy Spirit. We learn from St. Paul, however, that every Christian receives charisms: "To each is given the manifestation of the Spirit for the common good" (1 Corinthians 12:7). In the letters of St. Paul, it is clear that he simply assumes that each Christian has charisms and is using them.

Scholars of theology and history confirm that this same expectation was very much alive in the early Church, as evidenced by the Church Fathers and bishops who carried on the ministry of the apostles:

> The Church Fathers provide evidence of a broad pattern of expectation of charisms and the dynamic action of the Holy Spirit during Christian initiation (Baptism, Confirmation, and Eucharist). This pattern extends across various cultures, languages, geographical areas, ecclesiastical traditions and historical periods.[21]

Does Everyone Receive the Same Charisms?

"Unlike the fundamental graces such as sanctifying grace, or the gifts of faith, of hope, and of charity, that are indispensable for every Christian, an individual charism need not be a gift given to all."[22]

St. Paul teaches that:

> For to one is given through the Spirit the utterance of wisdom, and to another the utterance of knowledge according to the same Spirit, to another faith by the same Spirit, to another gifts of healing by the one Spirit, to another the working of miracles, to another prophecy, to another the ability to distinguish between spirits, to another various kinds of tongues, to another the interpretation of tongues. All these are empowered by one and the same Spirit, who apportions to each one individually as he wills. (1 Corinthians 12: 8-11)

Later he asks the rhetorical questions: "Do all possess gifts of healing? Do all speak with tongues? Do all interpret?" (1 Corinthians 12:30). Different Christians are given different charisms according to the plan and purposes of God.

CHAPTER TWO

How Are Charisms Related to the Seven Gifts of the Holy Spirit?

God gives many gifts to strengthen us, equip us, and empower us for good works. The seven gifts of the Holy Spirit received in Baptism and strengthened in Confirmation (wisdom, understanding, counsel, fortitude, knowledge, piety, and fear of the Lord) are harmoniously related to the charisms, but these seven gifts and the charisms serve different purposes.[23] The easiest way to understand the distinction is that "there are gifts of the Holy Spirit that we are given to keep and gifts we are given to give away. The traditional 'seven gifts of the Holy Spirit'. . . are gifts given to us to keep."[24] Often referred to as the Isaiah gifts, they sustain an individual Christian in virtue and docility to the Holy Spirit. The *Catechism* describes them in the following manner:

> The moral life of Christians is sustained by the gifts of the Holy Spirit. These are permanent dispositions which make man docile in following the promptings of the Holy Spirit.

The seven *gifts* of the Holy Spirit . . . belong in their fullness to Christ, Son of David. They complete and perfect the virtues of those who receive them. They make the faithful docile in readily obeying divine inspirations. (1830–1831)

These seven gifts of the Holy Spirit

are part of our inner transformation as Christians and provide the inner 'Christlikeness' necessary for the effective use of our charisms. . . . Charisms, on the other hand, are given to us to give away, and are one of the ways God continues to enter the world through our assent and cooperation. They always benefit other people.[25]

They are given "for the common good" (1 Corinthians 12:7), to equip people for works of service so that the body of Christ may be built up (see Ephesians 4:12). The *Catechism* confirms this important distinction:

Whether extraordinary or simple and humble, charisms are graces of the Holy Spirit which directly or indirectly benefit the Church, ordered as they are to her building up, to the good of men, and to the needs of the world. (799)

For this reason, they are often referred to as ministry gifts.

A simple analogy may help. The Isaiah gifts are like the rudder and sails on a sailing vessel. They allow a disciple to move effectively with the wind of the Holy Spirit. Charisms are like specialized equipment on the different vessels that allow each of them to fulfill their function in the larger fleet, such as transport ships, battleships, frigates, exploration ships, merchant ships, or reconnaissance ships. They uniquely equip each ship for action.

It is not surprising that charisms become more pronounced in areas and in ministries where the Church is being actively built up by evangelization and charitable outreach. And the greater the trials to advance the kingdom of God, the more likely the extraordinary charisms will be in evidence. As St. Thomas Aquinas pointed out, they exist precisely to empower missionaries with extraordinary knowledge of divine things, demonstrate and confirm the divine origin of the message of the gospel, and empower the minister to efficiently present the divine doctrine to those listening.[26]

Not surprisingly, the charisms are far less apparent in closed and static groups. This should remind us that

> They are not an inheritance, safely secured and entrusted to a small group for safekeeping; rather they are gifts of the Spirit integrated into the body of the Church, drawn to the center which is Christ and then channelled into an evangelizing impulse.[27]

As St. Basil the Great insisted,

> These gifts [charisms] are received by each one more for others than for themselves. . . . In the common life it is necessary that the power of the Holy Spirit, given to one, be transmitted to all. The one who lives for oneself may have a charism, but it remains useless, hidden away inactive, because it remains buried within the self."[28]

Why Do We Receive Different Charisms?

Charisms are distributed to the faithful "for the common good" (1 Corinthians 12:7), and this is why different charisms are given to different Christians: each of the faithful has a different function or mission within the mystical body of Christ (see 1 Corinthians 12:19-20). St. Paul explains this by analogy of the human body:

> For as in one body we have many members, and the members do not
> all have the same function, so we, though many, are one body in Christ,
> and individually members one of another. Having gifts that differ
> according to the grace given to us, let us use them. (Romans 12:4-6)

Charisms allow us to be channels of God's loving power and to
take on the mission of Christ in our own life, within our unique vocation and state of life. As the *Catechism* states, "Grace also includes the
gifts that the Spirit grants us to associate us with his work, to enable
us to collaborate in the salvation of others and in the growth of the
Body of Christ, the Church" (2003). The specific charisms the Spirit
allots to a person reveal how God wants to use them to build up the
Church and meet the needs of the world. This is precisely why it is
important to understand which charisms God has bestowed on us.

This reality cannot be overemphasized. Too many believe that the
laity are called only to be recipients of ministry, to do no more than
"pray, pay, and obey." Others mistakenly believe that to be active in
the Church means to volunteer for a service that is exercised entirely
within the four walls of the parish building. To the contrary,

> These faithful are by baptism made one body with Christ and are con-
> stituted among the People of God; they are in their own way made
> sharers in the priestly, prophetical, and kingly functions of Christ; and
> they carry out for their own part the mission of the whole Christian
> people in the Church and in the world."[29]

We are all called to mission by Baptism, not by virtue of ordina-
tion or consecration: "To be Christians means to be missionaries,
to be apostles. It is not enough to discover Christ—you must bring
him to others!"[30]

Certainly, collaboration with the clergy for ministry needs within
the Church is necessary,[31] but the lay apostolate is primarily secular in

character. This means that the lay mission is primarily in the world:

> [The laity bear] consistent witness in their personal, family, and social lives by proclaiming and sharing the Gospel of Christ in every situation in which they find themselves, and by their involvement with the task of explaining, defending, and correctly applying Christian principles to the problems of today's world."[32]

In this way, and in communion with the bishops, the lay faithful are coresponsible for the mission of the Church.[33] One of the critical ways they fulfill this mission is by the exercise of the charisms the Holy Spirit has given them.[34] The Decree on the Apostolate of the Laity, of the Second Vatican Council, made this explicit:

> The Holy Spirit Who sanctifies the people of God through ministry and the sacraments gives the faithful special gifts also (cf. 1 Cor. 12:7), "allotting them to everyone as He wills" (1 Cor. 12:11) ... to build up the whole body in charity (cf. Eph. 4:16). From the acceptance of these charisms, including those which as the most elementary, there arise for each believer the right and duty to use them in the Church and in the world for the good of men and the building up of the Church, in the freedom of the Holy Spirit who "breathes where He wills" (John 3:8).[35]

The Holy Spirit's distribution of charisms within the body of Christ also reveals the loving providence of God, for "wherever there is a particular need, he has already poured out the charisms that can meet it."[36] When there is a need in the Church, particularly in the service of her mission, the Holy Spirit provides members of the Church with the charisms necessary to meet that need.

St. Irenaeus of Lyon, an early Church Father and Doctor of the Church, who spoke of the Spirit making the Church "ever young and fresh, fruitful with multiple charisms,"[37] insisted on the need for each Christian to receive and use these gifts of the Holy Spirit. He strongly reproached and corrected those who relied only on the gifts of others.[38] The Church continues to teach that the faithful have a duty to use the charisms they receive in the Church and in the world.[39]

CHAPTER THREE

Were the Charisms Only for the Early Church?

When we read the Acts of the Apostles and the New Testament letters of the apostles and their coworkers, as well as the writings of the Church Fathers, we can easily see that the Pentecost experience of the Holy Spirit and his charisms permeated the life of the early Church. Some have speculated that this wonderful gift of the Holy Spirit was only for the time of the apostles in order to launch the Church. They believe that God does not bestow charisms anymore because they are no longer necessary. This contention is generally identified as cessationism, and it is not in accord with settled Catholic teaching.[40]

It is true, however, that there was an apparent decline in the use of the charisms after about the end of the fourth century. Many reasons have been proposed for this decline: lack of theological reflection on the Holy Spirit in the early Church; an overreaction to Montanism (a heresy that placed exaggerated importance on charisms over apostolic authority); the separation of the experience of Pentecost from Christian initiation through the new prevalence of infant baptism; the influx of converts who were less fervent and committed to their faith; the growing association of prophetic gifts with the visible hierarchy; the popular but incorrect view that charisms were restricted to the heights of holiness and monasticism; and the successful evangelization of Europe. All these factors likely played some part in the idea that the gifts were not as needed as they were during the time of expansion and confrontation with paganism.

Nevertheless, the charisms did not disappear from the experience of the Church altogether. Undoubtedly, the seemingly more ordinary charisms continued to operate during the times of Christian ascendency. As the more extraordinary charisms declined in use, however, attention to the charisms also declined. Though it was no longer a common expectation to manifest the charisms, a close look at history reveals that they were still very much in evidence:

> If we retrace the history of the Church, keeping in mind the various lists of charisms in the New Testament, we have to conclude that . . . none of the charisms was ever completely lost. The history of the Church is full of charismatic evangelizers, gifts of wisdom and knowledge (we only need to think of the Doctors of the Church), miraculous healings, people gifted with the spirit of prophecy or discernment of spirits, not to mention gifts such as visions, raptures, ecstasies, and illuminations that are also listed among the charisms.[41]

More widespread effusions of the Holy Spirit among the people of God were not unknown. Indeed, "One looking back at the history of the Church will be able to observe with gratitude that it has managed time and again in spite of all difficulties to make room for the great new awakenings."[42]

The nature and ongoing presence of charisms of the Holy Spirit—and the continuing need for these charisms—punctuate the mission-oriented documents of the most recent Ecumenical Council: the dogmatic constitution *Lumen Gentium* (Dogmatic Constitution on the Church) and the decrees *Apostolicam Actuositatem* (Decree on the Apostolate of the Laity), *Ad Gentes* (Decree on Missionary Activity), and *Presbyterorum Ordinis* (Decree on the Ministry and Life of Priests).

Is There a Special Need for Charisms Today?

Pope St. John XXIII inaugurated the Second Vatican Council by beseeching the Holy Spirit to "renew your wonders in this our day, as by a new Pentecost."[43] Shortly after the close of the council, there was a historical effusion of the charisms in the Church in several places throughout the world. It spread quickly and began to be referred to as a New Pentecost, or as a Charismatic Renewal. The extraordinary importance of this historical grace cannot be stressed strongly enough. It was enormously providential because it was desperately needed at this decisive period in the history of the Church. What we are presently experiencing is "not an age of change, but a change of the ages."[44]

As Archbishop Fulton Sheen said in 1974,

We are at the end of Christendom. Not of Christianity, not of the Church, but of Christendom. Now what is meant by Christendom? Christendom is economic, political, social life as inspired by Christian principles. That is ending—we've seen it die.[45]

After more than a millennium, Christendom no longer exists. As Pope St. John Paul II confirmed,

Even in countries evangelized many centuries ago, the reality of a "Christian society" which, amid all the frailties which have always marked human life, measured itself explicitly on Gospel values, is now gone.[46]

The effects are increasingly apparent:

> The real problem at this moment of our history is that God is disappearing from the human horizon, and, with the dimming of the light which comes from God, humanity is losing its bearings, with increasingly evident destructive effects.[47]

With the recent collapse of Christendom, the Church has entered a new apostolic age. The pastoral realities it faces are closer to those of the early Church than those of the recent past. In our new reality, the mission of the Church is clear:

> In our days, when in vast areas of the world the faith is in danger of dying out like a flame which no longer has fuel, the overriding priority is to make God present in this world and to show men and women the way to God. Not just any god, but the God who spoke on Sinai; to that God whose face we recognize in a love which presses "to the end" (cf. Jn 13:1)—in Jesus Christ, crucified and risen.[48]

What do we need? According to Pope Francis, we need

> a missionary impulse capable of transforming everything, so that the Church's customs, ways of doing things, times and schedules, language and structures can be suitably channeled for the evangelization of today's world rather than for her self-preservation.[49]

We must embrace this pastoral conversion and daunting mission with the steadfast faith and unwavering hope so powerfully expressed by Archbishop Sheen:

> These are great and wonderful days to be alive. . . . It is not a gloomy picture—it is a picture of the Church in the midst of increasing opposition

from the world. And therefore, live your lives in the full consciousness of this hour of testing, and rally close to the heart of Christ.[50]

In addition, we must also acknowledge that the challenge is insurmountable without "a new outpouring of the gift of God."[51]

In reality, the Church in many countries is dying. At this crucial moment of history, when "the peoples who have not yet received an initial proclamation of Christ constitute the majority of humanity,"[52] the God of Pentecost has provided a fresh outpouring of the Holy Spirit, accompanied by rich and varied ministry charisms to guide the Church, empower it, and give witness to the kingdom of God. Just as the mission of the apostles was launched and empowered by Pentecost, our mission in this new age of evangelization must be as well. It is the Holy Spirit who "grants the courage to proclaim the newness of the Gospel with boldness *(parrhesia)* in every time and place, even when it meets with opposition."[53] It is by "walking in the fear of the Lord and in the comfort of the Holy Spirit" that the Church is multiplied (Acts 9:31).

As Pope Francis declared to the Church in Canada, "We need to return to the simplicity and enthusiasm of the Acts of the Apostles, to the beauty of realizing that we are instruments of the Spirit's fruitfulness today."[54]

What Have the Popes Said about the Charisms in Our Time?

Pope St. John XXIII's successors have often spoken of the authenticity of this effusion of gifts, the need for the charisms, and the need for radical openness to this move of the Holy Spirit in our time. These are but a sampling of many such validations and exhortations.

Pope St. Paul VI asserted the following:

Nothing is more necessary to this more and more secularized world than the witness of the "spiritual renewal" that we see the Holy Spirit evoking in the most diverse regions and milieux. . . . How then could this "spiritual renewal" not be a "chance" for the Church and for the world? And how, in this case could one not take all the means to ensure that it remains so?[55]

[This charismatic renewal] ought to rejuvenate the world, give it back a spirituality, a soul, religious thought. It ought to reopen its closed lips to prayer and open its mouth to song, to joy, to hymns and to witnessing. It will be very fortuitous for our times, for our brothers, that there should be a generation, your generation of young people, who shout out to the world the glory and the greatness of the God of Pentecost.[56]

Assuredly we have here a work of the Spirit, a gift of Pentecost. One must also recognize a prophetic intuition on the part of our predecessor John XXIII, who envisaged a kind of new Pentecost as a fruit of the Council. We too have wished to place ourself in the same perspective and in the same attitude of expectation. Not that Pentecost has ever ceased to be an actuality during the whole history of the Church, but so great are the needs and the perils of the present age, so vast the horizon of mankind drawn towards world coexistence and powerless to achieve it, that there is no salvation for it except in a new outpouring of the gift of God.[57]

Pope St. John Paul II also recognized the providence of God in this renewal of charisms in the Church.

I am convinced that this [charismatic renewal] movement is a very important component of the entire renewal of the Church. . . . I can understand all these different charisms. They are all part of the richness of the Lord. I am convinced that this movement is a sign of his action![58]

The Spirit has guided the church in every age, producing a great variety of gifts among the faithful. Because of the Spirit, the church preserves a continual youthful vitality, and the charismatic renewal is an eloquent manifestation of this today, a bold statement of what the Spirit is saying to the churches (Rv. 2:7).[59]

How can we not give thanks for the precious spiritual fruits that the Renewal has produced in the life of the Church and in the lives of so many people? How many lay faithful—men, women, young people, adults and the elderly—have been able to experience in their own lives the amazing power of the Spirit and his gifts! How many people have rediscovered the faith, the joy of prayer, the power and beauty of the Word of God, translating all this into generous service in the Church's mission! How many lives have been profoundly changed! For all this today, together with you, I wish to praise and thank the Holy Spirit.[60]

At this moment in the Church's history, the Charismatic Renewal can play a significant role in promoting the much-needed defense of Christian life in societies where secularism and materialism have weakened many people's ability to respond to the Spirit and to discern God's loving call. Your contribution to the re-evangelization of society will be made in the first place by personal witness to the indwelling Spirit and by showing forth His presence through works of holiness and solidarity.[61]

Thanks to the Charismatic Movement, a multitude of Christians, men and women, young people and adults, have rediscovered Pentecost as a living reality in their daily lives. I hope that the spirituality of Pentecost will spread in the Church as a renewed incentive to prayer, holiness, communion and proclamation.[62]

Today, I would like to cry out to all of you . . . and to all Christians: Open yourselves docilely to the gifts of the Spirit! Accept gratefully and obediently the charisms which the Spirit never ceases to bestow on us! Do not forget that every charism is given for the common good, that is, for the benefit of the whole Church.[63]

Pope Benedict XVI likewise saw the hand of God in this renewal, both as Prefect of the Congregation for the Doctrine of the Faith and later as pope.

What is emerging here is a new generation of the Church which I am watching with great hope. I find it marvelous that the Spirit is once more stronger than our programs and brings himself into play in an altogether different way than we had imagined. . . . Our task—the task of the office-holders in the Church and of theologians—is to keep the door open to them, to prepare room for them.[64]

The period following the Council scarcely seemed to live up to the hopes of John XXIII, who looked for a "new Pentecost." But his prayer did not go unheard. In the heart of a world desiccated by rationalistic skepticism, a new experience of the Holy Spirit has come about, amounting to a worldwide renewal movement. What the New Testament describes, with reference to the charisms, as visible signs of the coming of the Spirit is no longer merely ancient, past history: this history is becoming a burning reality today.[65]

I am really a friend of . . . the Charismatic Renewal. I think this is a sign of the Springtime and of the presence of the Holy Spirit, [who] today will give new charisms and so on. This is for me really a great hope that not with organization from authorities, but really it is the force of the Holy Spirit present in the people.[66]

At this point, to avoid misunderstandings, it should be said quite clearly that the apostolic movements appear in ever new forms in history—necessarily so, because they are the Holy Spirit's answer to the ever-changing situations in which the Church lives. And just as vocations to the priesthood cannot be artificially produced, cannot be established by administrative diktat, still less can movements be established and systematically promoted by ecclesiastical authority. They need to be given as a gift, and they are given as a gift. We must only be attentive to them. Using the gift of discernment, we must only learn to accept what is good in them, and discard what is bad. . . . What, in the last analysis, needs to be established is not a blasé attitude of intellectual superiority that immediately brands the zeal of those seized by the Holy Spirit and their uninhibited faith with the anathema of fundamentalism, and only authorises a faith in which the ifs and buts are more important than the substance of what is believed.[67]

What we learn in the New Testament on charisms, which appeared as visible signs of the coming of the Holy Spirit, is not a historical event of the past, but a reality ever alive. It is the same divine Spirit, soul of the Church, that acts in every age and those mysterious and effective interventions of the Spirit are manifest in our time in a providential way.[68]

Let us ask the Virgin Mary to obtain . . . a renewed Pentecost for the Church that will imbue in all, and especially in the young, the joy of living and witnessing to the Gospel.[69]

Pope Francis has echoed his predecessors in blessing and affirming this global spiritual renewal as an action of the Holy Spirit:

You, the charismatic renewal, have received a great gift from the Lord. Your movement's birth was willed by the Holy Spirit to be "a current of grace in the Church and for the Church." This is your identity: to be a current of grace. . . .

You have received the great gift of diversity of charisms, the diversity which becomes harmony in the Holy Spirit, in service to the Church. . . .

The Charismatic Renewal is a great force meant to serve the preaching of the Gospel in the joy of the Holy Spirit. . . .

You, the people of God, the people of the Charismatic Renewal, must be careful not to lose the freedom which the Holy Spirit has given you! . . .

I expect you to share with everyone in the Church the grace of baptism in the Holy Spirit (a phrase we find in the Acts of the Apostles)."[70]

Is This Renewal Merely a Single Movement among Many Movements in the Church?

Pope Francis addressed this question during a talk to members of the Charismatic Renewal. He did so by quoting a homily that Cardinal Leon-Joseph Suenens—one of the early advocates of this current of grace—gave in the presence of Pope St. Paul VI. Pope Francis quoted the cardinal who said:

May the Charismatic Renewal disappear as such and be transformed into a Pentecostal grace for the whole Church: to be faithful to its origin, the river must lose itself in the ocean. . . . The first error that must be avoided is including the Charismatic Renewal in the category of Movement. It is not a specific Movement; the Renewal is not a Movement in the common sociological sense; it does not have founders, it is not homogeneous and it includes a great variety of realities; it is a current of grace, a renewing breath of the Spirit for all members of the Church, laity, religious, priests and bishops. It is a challenge for us all. One does not form part of the Renewal, rather, the Renewal becomes a part of us provided that we accept the grace it offers us.[71]

While the word "movement" is still often applied to this effusion of charisms in the Church, it is clearly used in a unique manner. It is a current of grace rather than a particular defined program, devotion, or community. Cardinal Raniero Cantalamessa, OFM Cap, emphasizes this important distinction simply and clearly: "The Charismatic Renewal is a current of grace that is necessary for the whole Catholic Church."[72]

CHAPTER FOUR

Does the Church Have any Cautions about the Use of Charisms?

The Fathers of the Second Vatican Council gave the following cautions regarding charisms:

> Extraordinary gifts are not to be sought after, nor are the fruits of apostolic labor to be presumptuously expected from their use; but judgment as to their genuinity and proper use belongs to those who are appointed leaders in the Church, to whose special competence it belongs, not indeed to extinguish the Spirit, but to test all things and hold fast to that which is good (1 Th. 5:12, 19-21).[73]

The first caution has to do with rashly desiring gifts. St. Paul tells us that we should "earnestly desire the greater gifts" (1 Corinthians 12:31), but to be rash is to act impetuously or without careful consideration of the possible consequences. As we have seen, the gift of a charism comes with a serious responsibility to use it with sacrificial love for others. Exercising charisms may at times require courage and may test one's faith, stretch one's love, and cause personal trials.

The greater our fidelity to the Gospel mission, the greater our experience of the Beatitudes (see Matthew 5:1-12). We should desire greater gifts, but with profound humility and serious commitment.

The second caution is against the presumption that we will necessarily receive spiritual fruits by the mere exercise of charisms. Presumption is a serious offense against God because it treats his gifts as though they were automatic—more like magic than grace. Charisms cannot substitute for the sacramental life of the Church, growth in holiness, or collaboration with grace as we apply our reason and will to the mission. Nor can it substitute for the love of God and neighbor at the heart of every authentic apostolate. "Even the most powerful charisms do not exempt Christians from taking up the cross and embracing the cost of discipleship."[74]

Charisms must also be exercised with trust and humble surrender: "For as the heavens are higher than the earth, so are my ways higher than your ways and my thoughts than your thoughts" (Isaiah 55:9). God's will, not our own, must be our deepest desire.

The final caution has to do with discernment and proper authority. God has given those who hold offices of authority in the Church the responsibility to test all things and ensure that charisms are genuine and that they are being exercised properly.

> Paul teaches . . . that God has established a hierarchy in the Church (cf. [1 Corinthians] 12:28): first come the "apostles," then the "prophets," then the "teachers." These three positions are fundamental and are listed in order of importance.[75]

Mature humility, openness to guidance and correction, and responsible obedience are positive signs of authenticity.

The misuse of charisms, as with any gift or responsibility, is always possible. Indeed, in the early days of the renewal, there was a certain immaturity in the use of gifts and a lack of integration with the fullness of Catholic life and spirituality. Similar issues can occur today. But we should not let the misuse of such a powerful grace from God lead to its repudiation. The Church herself teaches the proper attitude we should foster toward charisms:

> Charisms are to be accepted with gratitude by the person who receives them and by all members of the Church as well. They are a wonderfully rich grace for the apostolic vitality and for the holiness of the entire Body of Christ, provided they really are genuine gifts of the Holy Spirit and are used in full conformity with authentic promptings of this same Spirit, that is, in keeping with charity, the true measure of all charisms. (*Catechism*, 800)

How Do the Institution of the Church and the Charisms Work Together?

The teaching of the Second Vatican Council—reflecting the Scriptures and building on the teaching of Pope Pius XII[76]—"reveal in the life of the Church, in addition to the Word of God, written and transmitted, to the sacraments, and to the ordained hierarchical ministry, the presence of gifts, of special gifts or charisms, distributed by the Spirit among the faithful of every condition."[77]

The council declared,

> The Church, which the Spirit guides in the way of all truth (cf. Jn. 16:13) and which He unifies in communion and in works of ministry, He both equips and directs with hierarchical and charismatic gifts and adorns with His fruits (cf. Eph. 4:11-12, 1 Cor. 12:4, Gal 5:22).[78]

Pope St. John Paul II highlighted this significantly in his 1998 Pentecost homily:

The institutional and charismatic aspects are co-essential as it were to the Church's constitution. They contribute, although differently, to the life, renewal and sanctification of God's people.[79]

At a subsequent Wednesday audience, he illustrated how the "New Testament testifies to the presence of charisms and ministries inspired by the Holy Spirit in the various Christian communities." Using the example of the church at Antioch, he noted that

[what] clearly emerges [is] the twofold method with which the Spirit of God governs the Church: on the one hand, he directly encourages the activity of believers by revealing new and unprecedented ways to proclaim the Gospel, on the other, he provides an authentication of their work through the official intervention of the Church, represented here by the work of Barnabas, who was sent by the mother community of Jerusalem.[80]

It is crucial that we understand this relationship between the hierarchical and the charismatic gifts in the life and mission of the Church. Without it, we cannot fully cooperate with the work of the Holy Spirit in and through the Church. The institutional and charismatic dimensions of the Church are meant to work together, a bit like a river within its banks. A river is not a river unless it has both effective banks and moving water, just as the Church is not the Church unless it has both its institutional and charismatic dimensions.

We need the banks of the river. They direct the power of the river in the right direction, into its correct course. Without proper banks, a river can easily become a treacherous flood and cause considerably more damage than good. In the same way, we need the institution of the Church: "The one mediator, Christ, established and ever sustains here on earth his holy Church, the community of faith, hope, and charity, as a visible organization through which he communicates truth and grace to all men" (*Catechism*, 771).

"Christ governs her through Peter and the other apostles, who are present in their successors, the pope and the college of bishops" (*Catechism*, 869). This, too, is a great gift of God,[81] and it is for this reason that "those who have charge over the Church should judge the genuineness and proper use of these gifts."[82] The institutional dimension of the Church must safeguard and ensure the correct course of the charismatic dimension. But it must be exceedingly clear that "it is not the Spirit who is in service to the institution, but the institution that is in service to the Spirit."[83]

The dangers of neglecting the pastoral authority of the hierarchy, especially of its teaching office, have been all too evident in history. To give just a few examples, Montanism was an early movement with a false understanding and practice of prophecy[84] and was "characterized by abuses and excesses in the use of charisms."[85] It caused deep division and confusion within the Church and carried many away from the unity of Faith, and its last adherents weren't reconciled until the fifth century under St. Augustine. Illuminism is another spiritually dangerous movement that claims, in part, that personal divine enlightenment is more authoritative than the Church's Magisterium or even the Deposit of Faith.[86] It has plagued the Church in different guises since the early sixteenth century.

Two other dangers associated with spiritual charisms are the temptation to think of them as marks of holiness and the coveting of spiritual authority over others. Certainly, the exercise of charisms in charity will bring about an increase in sanctity, but their presence does not indicate holiness as some mystical gifts do. The misguided use of authority among a few spiritual leaders of the renewal has been a more recent concern for the Church.[87] If authority is not exercised with charity, detachment, and humility, it is not to God's glory. One can see why the "discernment of charisms is always necessary. No charism is exempt from being referred and submitted to the Church's shepherds" (*Catechism*, 801).

We also need the rushing water. As critical as they are, the banks of a river are no more than a dry ditch if there is no water, or boundaries of a stagnant pond if the water is not moving. It may appear orderly and even scenic, but there is no movement or power. In a similar way, the gospel advances, the Church is built up, and the common good is realized by the exciting power of the Holy Spirit at work in the lives of Christians (see *Catechism*, 2003).

It is a grave mistake to think that the gospel mission can advance without the dynamic working of the Holy Spirit in and through individual disciples of Jesus. Institutional planning, strategic thinking, and human efforts are critically necessary, but alone they are not enough. They must be informed by, and empowered by, the Holy Spirit. As Pope St. Paul VI reminded us,

> Techniques of evangelization are good, but even the most advanced ones could not replace the gentle action of the Spirit. The most perfect preparation of the evangelizer has no effect without the Holy Spirit. Without the Holy Spirit the most convincing dialectic has no power over the heart of man. Without Him the most highly developed schemas resting on a sociological or psychological basis are quickly seen to be quite valueless.[88]

Cardinal Joseph Ratzinger, then Prefect of the Congregation of the Doctrine of the Faith, made this point boldly:

> [The local Churches] must not turn their own pastoral plans into the criterion of what the Holy Spirit is allowed to do: an obsession with planning could render the Churches impervious to the action of the Holy Spirit, to the power of God by which they live. Not everything

should be fitted into the straightjacket of a single uniform organization; what is needed is less organization and more Spirit![89]

We must remain docile and open to the impulse of the Holy Spirit. As Pope St. John Paul II asserted, "Whenever the Spirit intervenes, he leaves people astonished. He brings about events of amazing newness; he radically changes persons and history."[90] It is because of the charisms that "the people of God are able fully to live their evangelical mission, discerning the signs of the times and interpreting them in the light of the Gospel."[91]

It is imperative that we have expectant faith and responsive hearts because charisms "manifest the creativity of the Spirit and are given generously and often beyond all expectations."[92]

Some charisms given by the Spirit burst in like an impetuous wind, which seizes people and carries them to new ways of missionary commitment to the radical service of the Gospel, by ceaselessly proclaiming the truths of faith, accepting the living stream of tradition as a gift and instilling in each person an ardent desire for holiness.[93]

As the Congregation of the Doctrine of the Faith has noted,

The charismatic gifts, in fact, enable the faithful to respond to the gift of salvation in complete freedom and in a way suited to the times. In this way, they themselves become a gift of love for others and authentic witnesses to the Gospel before all mankind.[94]

We must never "put the Holy Spirit in a cage!"[95] It is important to recognize, however, that unleashing the Holy Spirit will likely disrupt the seemingly peaceful order and tranquil decline of the Church. His action can make things messy as he invades individual lives, ministries, and parishes. Rushing water can be turbulent. At times this may prove to be pastorally demanding and take us out of our comfort zones, but it is the price of authentic docility to the revitalizing power of the Holy Spirit.

Analogies such as the river and its banks are helpful, but also limited. It is important to recognize that the institutional and charismatic aspects of the Church are not wholly distinct realities, but rather deeply integrated. Indeed, those who exercise offices of authority in the Church have also been given charisms and may have received others by virtue of their office. As Cardinal St. John Newman recognized, "The heart of every Christian ought to represent in miniature the Catholic Church, since one Spirit makes both the whole Church and every member of it to be His Temple."[96]

In summary,

> the relationship between the charismatic gifts and the ecclesial sacramental structure confirms the coessentiality between hierarchical gifts—of their nature stable, permanent, and irrevocable—and the charismatic gifts. Even if the historical forms of the latter are not guaranteed to remain always the same, nonetheless the charismatic dimension will never be lacking in the life and mission of the Church.[97]

St. Irenaeus summed this up concisely: "For where the Church is, there also is God's Spirit; where God's Spirit is, there is the Church and every grace" (*Catechism*, 797).

CHAPTER FIVE

Can There Be Contradictions between the Institution of the Church and the Charisms?

As Pope St. John Paul II has stressed,

> The Apostle [Paul] . . . teaches that the diversity of charisms must not create divisions, and for this reason compares them to the various members of the one body (cf. [1 Cor.] 12:12-27). The Church's unity is dynamic and organic, and all the gifts of the Spirit are important for the vitality of the Body as a whole. . . .
>
> [T]here is no such thing as one Church according to a "charismatic model" and another according to an "institutional model." As I have had the opportunity to stress on other occasions, opposition between charism and institution is "extremely harmful."[98]

At certain times, however, there may be tension between these two coessential aspects of the Church. The exercise of charisms can challenge the institutional status quo, especially when the status quo urgently needs reform and renewal. It can even cause disruption if the salt has lost its savor because "the local Churches may have entered into a kind of conformist *modus vivendi* with the world."[99] Holy discontent and agitation for personal and institutional conversion is itself a work of the Holy Spirit.

The whole Church, especially its shepherds, must be attentive and humbly obedient to the sometimes painful but purifying action of the Holy Spirit. We must remain vigilant and never "quench the Spirit" (1 Thessalonians 5:19) when in his infinite love he convicts us of "sin and righteousness and judgement" (John 16:8). Likewise, correction or course adjustment over the theology or exercise of charisms required by the hierarchy of the Church can be difficult for unintentionally erring disciples. But the shepherds have been charged to guard the Deposit of Faith (see 1 Timothy 6:20) and will be held accountable (see Hebrews 13:17).

Both forms of correction are occasionally necessary, and both are the guiding hand of a faithful God. The Spirit is like the wind (see John 3:8), and he is present both in the powerful and stable jet stream of Scripture, Tradition, and Magisterium, and in the insistent gusts summoning and mobilizing individuals to action. There can be no real contradiction, or mere juxtaposition, of the hierarchical and charismatic gifts.[100] "Both dimensions originate from the same Holy Spirit for the same Body of Christ, and together they concur to make present the mystery and the salvific work of Christ in the world."[101]

All the faithful, regardless of their office or vocation, must remain docile to the guidance and correction of the Holy Spirit. This is especially true when there are tensions, trials, and challenges. Proper discernment is always required and should be welcomed with an openness to the often-surprising ways of the Holy Spirit.[102] St. Clement of Alexandria warned that to fail to follow the Spirit's transforming lead is injustice to the Holy Spirit, and he likens it to imprisonment of the Holy Spirit.[103]

What Are the Criteria for Discerning Charismatic Gifts?

There are certain clear criteria in the Sacred Scriptures by which we can discern both the authenticity and the authentic exercise of a spiritual charism:

1. The manifestation of a charism, as well as any guidance or knowledge received through the exercise of a charism, must be in conformity with the Deposit of Faith (see 1 Timothy 6:20; 2 John 9).
2. Those exercising charisms must demonstrate humility, as well as mature and responsible obedience to those exercising pastoral authority over them (see Hebrews 13:17; 1 Peter 5:5).
3. Charity must be the intentional goal and measure of the exercise of every charism (see 1 Corinthians 13).
4. An authentic charism must be for the common good so that the body of Christ may be built up (see 1 Corinthians 12:7; Ephesians 4:12).
5. The exercise of a charism must be ordered to unity and charity within the Church (see 1 Corinthians 12:12-26).
6. The exercise of a charism must be in conformity with the fruits of the Spirit, and not of the flesh (see Galatians 5:16-26).
7. Authentic charisms bear good supernatural fruit (see John 15:5; Matthew 7:17).
8. A charism "is not genuine unless it leads to proclaiming that Jesus Christ is Lord" (see 1 Corinthians 12:1-3).[104]

In referring to the exercise of charisms, St. Paul insists that "all things should be done decently and in order" (1 Corinthians 14:40). We are further instructed to "test the spirits to see whether they are from God" (1 John 4:1). Manifestations that are dehumanizing or tend toward the bizarre should be distrusted, carefully discerned, and properly addressed by those with the responsibility of leadership. Although new experiences of the Holy Spirit may be initially unfamiliar, authentic charisms of the Holy Spirit will always glorify God, uphold the dignity of persons, and build up the faith of unbelievers.

What Is the Role of the Church's Pastors in regard to the Charisms of the Faithful?

Cardinal Stanislaw Rylko, who served as President of the Pontifical Council for the Laity, summarized the responsibility of the pastors of the Church with regard to the charisms:

> One thing, however, is certain: the face of the Church of the third millennium depends on our capacity to listen to what the Spirit is saying to the Church of our time (cf. Rev 2:7). . . . It depends, therefore, on our capacity to be amazed by the charismatic gifts that the Holy Spirit is lavishing on the Church today with extraordinary generosity. And it depends on the wisdom and generous farsightedness of Pastors who do not quench the Spirit, but test everything and hold fast to what is good (cf. 1 Thes. 5:12, 19-21).[105]

Bishops, as shepherds of the faithful, are called to welcome and affirm the gifts of the laity, the initiatives of the Holy Spirit, and to "open themselves up to the new movements, create room for them in their local Churches, struggle patiently with them, . . . and guide them to the right form."[106] "It is the task of Pastors to discern the authenticity of charisms and to regulate their exercise in an attitude of humble obedience to the Spirit, of disinterested love for the Church's good and of docile fidelity to the supreme law of the salvation of souls."[107]

The priest, as a faithful collaborator of the bishop, is to "see to it . . . that the faithful are led individually in the Holy Spirit to a development of their own vocation according to the Gospel, to a sincere and practical charity."[108] More specifically,

> While trying the spirits to see if they be of God, priests should uncover with a sense of faith, acknowledge with joy and foster with diligence the various humble and exalted charisms of the laity.[109]

Furthermore,

> The priest, for his part, cannot exercise his service on behalf of the Renewal unless and until he adopts a welcoming attitude towards it, based on the desire he shares with every Christian by baptism to grow in the gifts of the Holy Spirit.[110]

To recognize and affirm the charisms of the lay faithful and to equip them for their apostolate is a critical part of what it means for a priest to govern the portion of the people of God entrusted to his leadership. In communion with his bishop and with the assistance of the deacons, parish leaders, and catechists, the local pastor must ensure that the whole people of God are mobilized for mission.

CHAPTER SIX

Why Should We Discern Which Charisms the Holy Spirit Has Allotted to Us?

Discerning which charisms the Holy Spirit has given to a person is extremely important. It reveals a vital aspect of God's plan for our life—namely, the mission to which God has called and equipped us. Embracing God's will by generously exercising the charisms he has bestowed on us is remarkably freeing, satisfying, and fulfilling. In addition,

> If you know your gifts, it becomes easier to say "no" when people ask you for things that you don't really have to give. And because it is unusually energizing and fulfilling to exercise a charism, you are much less likely to burn out if you are working in your area of giftedness.[111]

Discerning charisms also assists the local parish and allows us to look at our parishes in an entirely new way:

> Our communities are filled with organizational and pastoral needs that are usually met by recruiting anyone who shows any interest or

who, perhaps, is just unable to say "no." Because we seldom look first at the gifts and call of individuals, our communities too often contain generous and energetic people who have been burned-out or even traumatized trying to fill "vacuums" for which they were ill-equipped. But if we look first at our gifts, our communities will come to be shaped by our loves, because God calls each of us to (and gifts us for) the work that we most love.[112]

How Do We Know Which Charisms the Holy Spirit Has Allotted to Us?

There are three essential signs that indicate that a charism has been given to someone. The first is that they are energized when exercising a certain charism, almost as if something has come alive inside them. There is generally a sense of fulfillment and abiding joy. This is the interior data for discernment.

The other two forms of data are external. The second indicator of the presence of a charism is that people request it of you. People intuitively recognize when someone is gifted in a particular way and seek them out for assistance. People who exercise the gift of counsel, for example, often find themselves being sought out for their counsel; they don't need to convince anyone.

The final sign of the presence of a charism is that it works. We can see and experience the effects. When a person with the charism of healing prays with people, healing of one sort or another often occurs. When a person has the charism of teaching, those who receive the instruction experience it as more than just the transfer of knowledge; they experience the interior conviction of the Holy Spirit. In effect, people generally experience something singular or special, whether or not they can consciously identify it as the Holy Spirit.

Discerning a charism is best done with others and with the accompaniment of someone skilled in discerning charisms. Friends, fellow disciples, and qualified spiritual directors can tell us things we can't see ourselves and help us recognize charisms that we would have missed. In particular, someone trained in discerning charisms can also help us see the difference between charisms, natural talents, and acquired skills, and understand how these work together for we know that grace builds on nature.

How Are the Charisms Released More Fully in Our Lives?

Many people are operating in the charisms of the Holy Spirit in their everyday lives and apostolates without even recognizing it. This happens especially when the charism seems more ordinary and is part of a person's lived experience. Generally speaking, however, the discovery of charisms comes after someone has experienced a spiritual awakening, whether through a Cursillo, spiritual retreat, Alpha Course, CCO Discovery Faith Study, Life in the Spirit Seminar, The Rescue Project, or the like—in other words, after a "personal Pentecost," wherein a person experiences the Holy Spirit in a new way. It is this experience, with the deeper personal commitment to the Faith and the new discovery of charisms, that launches them into mission. There is an important lesson here.

Many Catholics today are puzzled by the following question: If, as our Faith assures us, we receive the Holy Spirit in Baptism and Confirmation, and his presence in us is strengthened in wonderful ways through the other sacraments, why do our lives look and feel exactly the same after we receive these sacraments? Why do so many newly baptized adults not notice any difference in their lives? Why do so many recently confirmed young adults stop practicing their faith altogether instead of becoming courageous witnesses to Jesus? Why do so many who go to Mass and receive the Blessed Sacrament—eating, along with it, as St. Ephrem so vividly said, "Fire and Spirit"[113]—do so in such a perfunctory manner with no apparent fruits? It is hard to imagine a more vital or pressing question.

In order to properly address this key question, we need to notice that the apostles experienced the very same problem. After Jesus had risen victoriously from the dead, we find the apostles hiding in fear (see John 20:19). Even after they had encountered the risen Lord, they still hid away by themselves (see 20:26). They looked exactly the same as they always had and were definitely not ready for the mission. They had no idea what to do, ... so they went back to fishing (see 21:3). They, too, had received the Holy Spirit. They had been baptized, had received Jesus in the Eucharist at the Last Supper, and had been ordained as priests in the Upper Room. And the risen Jesus had "breathed on them and said to them, 'Receive the Holy Spirit'" (20:22).[114] But they still needed something!

Jesus knew that they were not ready, and consequently, he did not immediately send them out on mission. He promised them something more, and he prepared them to receive it:

> He presented himself alive to them after his suffering by many proofs, appearing to them during forty days and speaking about the king-dom of God.
>
> And while staying with them he ordered them not to depart from Jerusalem, but to wait for the promise of the Father, which, he said, "you heard from me; for John baptized with water, but you will be baptized with the Holy Spirit not many days from now." (Acts 1:3-5)

After the ascension of Jesus, they did what he asked them to do. They "were devoting themselves to prayer, together with the women and Mary the mother of Jesus, and his brothers" (Acts 1:14). What Jesus had them praying, preparing, and waiting for became powerfully evident on the day of Pentecost. They "were all filled with the Holy Spirit," charisms manifested, and, as St. Peter explained, "This is what was uttered through the prophet Joel: 'And in the last days it shall be, God declares, that I will pour out a portion of my Spirit on all flesh'" (2:4, 16-17). "The Spirit of God was poured out in superabundance, like a cascade capable of purifying every heart, extinguishing the fire of evil, and kindling the flame of divine love in the world."[115]

The "something more" that Jesus had promised and instructed them to prepare for was what he himself called being "baptized with the Holy Spirit" (Acts 1:5). It transformed the apostles from confused and frightened men, hiding for their lives, into bold witnesses to all that they had seen and heard. They had three thousand converts that very first day. They went on to bring the gospel to the whole known world, just as Jesus had commanded them to do.

Being baptized in the Holy Spirit is not to be confused with the Sacrament of Baptism. "The Lord himself affirms that Baptism is necessary for salvation" (*Catechism*, 1257). By it we are given the Holy Spirit who communicates his divine life to us.

> Baptism not only purifies from all sins, but also makes the neophyte "a new creature," an adopted son of God, who has become a "partaker of the divine nature," member of Christ and co-heir with him, and a temple of the Holy Spirit. (*Catechism*, 1265)

Furthermore, "the reception of the sacrament of Confirmation is necessary for the completion of baptismal grace" (*Catechism*, 1285).

> By Confirmation Christians, that is, those who are anointed, share more completely in the mission of Jesus Christ and the fullness of the Holy Spirit with which he is filled, so that their lives may give off "the aroma of Christ." (*Catechism*, 1294)

The sacraments are irreplaceable. Being baptized in the Holy Spirit is something different. It is a grace that "helps to revivify the divine gifts received in sacramental Baptism" and brings "a quickening or an enlivening of faith which enables us to perceive divine realities in a new and life-giving way."[116] As we see in the life of the apostles, this effusion of the Holy Spirit may even be received more than once (see Acts 4:31). As St. Thomas Aquinas explains, there may be new sendings of the Spirit, particularly when there are special callings and missions.[117]

To clarify this distinction more precisely, it is important to understand that the Greek word *baptizo* simply means an immersion. The baptism in the Holy Spirit that the risen Jesus instructed the apostles to wait for and then poured out on them at Pentecost—and again in Jerusalem some time later (see Acts 4:31)—is a spiritual "washing," or immersion, in the Holy Spirit. Ideally, for those who are old enough, this happens when they receive the Sacraments of Initiation. But it may happen at a later period, especially, as we have seen, when someone is experiencing an awakening in their faith. Whenever it happens,

> [It is] a life-transforming experience of the love of God the Father poured into one's heart by the Holy Spirit, received through a surrender to the lordship of Jesus Christ. It brings alive sacramental Baptism and Confirmation, deepens communion with God and with fellow Christians, enkindles evangelistic fervour and equips a person with charisms for service and mission.[118]

The baptism in the Holy Spirit unleashes the Holy Spirit:

> [It] is a call to permanent conversion, as on the day of the Pentecostal descent of the Spirit in Jerusalem. It is a new awareness of the

Lordship of Jesus in our life, that Jesus who is Lord, and only through the Spirit can he be loved, adored, proclaimed, witnessed and shared.[119]

A provocative question attributed to the late Cardinal Suenens beautifully captures the difference that being baptized in the Holy Spirit makes: "You have the Holy Spirit, but does the Holy Spirit have you?"

People often receive this baptism in the Holy Spirit through prayer ministry and the laying on of hands, but the manner in which it is received doesn't matter. "Although the Spirit often comes in response to prayer, he comes in a way that is gratuitous, mysterious, and uniquely tailored to each individual."[120] What does matter is a heart opening to God. Jesus assures us that "if you then, who are evil, know how to give good gifts to your children, how much more will the heavenly Father give the Holy Spirit to those who ask him!" (Luke 11:13).

An important dynamic of opening one's life more fully to the Holy Spirit is the need to intentionally yield and respond to God's initiative:

> We have to say "Yes." If there is one word that's a key word in our relationship with God it is the word "yes." When we say "yes" to what Jesus calls us to, then the Spirit of God is stirred up within us. We receive God's Holy Spirit when we're baptized. We receive the Holy Spirit of God in fulness when we are confirmed. But God's Holy Spirit lays within us almost in a treasure chest, almost dormant until we begin consciously to respond and say "yes." When we do that, the Holy Spirit begins to well up within us, and that's what changes lives."[121]

As Sherry Weddell, creator of the Catholic Spiritual Gifts Inventory, affirms:

> Whether the experience is sudden and dramatic, or cumulative and quiet, the result is the same: you begin to seek God, to live as a disciple

of Christ, and to open yourself to being used by the Holy Spirit. This is the soil that allows the seeds of the charisms to come into full bloom.[122]

Does the Use of Charisms Require a Particular Vocation, Spirituality, or Expression?

Exercising charisms is for all Christians of all spiritual traditions, temperaments, personalities, vocations, and states of life. Nobody is excluded. Even silent contemplatives and hermits are called to exercise the charisms allotted to them just as surely as clergy and laypeople living and ministering in the midst of the world. The charisms they exercise may be different, but the call is the same.

Many who have experienced being baptized in the Holy Spirit display a joyful and exuberant expression of their faith, not unlike that described in the Old and New Testaments. This is often described as flowing from the joy of a deep personal encounter with the risen and living Jesus and from the abiding peace that only he can give (see John 14:27). Even people who are more naturally introverted often experience a new freedom in private prayer, public worship, and personal witness to their faith. For many people, this is a beautiful fruit of coming alive in the Holy Spirit, though it isn't any kind of requirement. For others of a more spiritually contemplative disposition, there is nonetheless an almost universal experience of profound inward joy, spiritual awakening, and enkindled zeal.

Expressions of joy, enthusiasm, and evangelical fervor born of the Holy Spirit are by no means absent in the history of the Church. Indeed, the Holy Spirit constantly raises up individual disciples and whole movements for reform and renewal. The entire history of the Church bears abounding witness to this. One example is the thirteenth-century revival brought about through the preaching of St. Francis of Assisi and his followers. One contemporary author described it this way:

It was a time of merriment and gladness, of joy and exultation, of praise and jubilation. During this time men of all sorts sang songs of praise to God. . . . Old people and young people were of one mind. This turning to God was experienced in all the cities of Italy, and they came from the villages to the town with banners, a great multitude of people, men and women, boys and girls together, to hear the preaching and to praise God. The songs that they sang were of God, not of man, and all walked in the way of salvation. . . . Sermons were preached in the evening, in the morning and at noon. . . . Men took their places in churches and outdoors and lifted up their hands to God, to praise and bless him forever and ever. They [wished] they would never have to stop praising God, they were so drunk with his love.[123]

There are some who distrust such enthusiastic expressions, fearing an overemphasis and overreliance on personal experience at the expense of clear doctrine. But this is a false dichotomy. We need both a deeply grounded informed faith and hearts fully alive to the living God. Indeed, "a dogmatic faith unsupported by personal experience remains empty; mere personal experience unrelated to the faith of the Church remains blind."[124] We sometimes need to be reminded that "being Christian is not the result of an ethical choice or a lofty idea, but the encounter with an event, a person, which gives life a new horizon and a decisive direction."[125]

Others express concern that overt fervor is unseemly or that it is mere emotionalism. Certainly there are situations in which this concern is merited, where prudence or human maturity is lacking. Nonetheless, authentic joy born of divine love should never be the object of suspicion. Indeed, "the disciples and all those who believe in Christ are called to share this joy. Jesus wishes them to have in themselves His joy in its fullness."[126] Faith is, after all, not merely an intellectual or volitional activity. It is also an emotional activity.[127]

St. Augustine made a spirited defense of emotions and affections, and considered an insensitivity to the touch of emotion the worst of all vices.[128] St. Thomas Aquinas taught that the more perfect a virtue is, the more passion it causes.[129] As St. Philip Neri said so eloquently, "Let us aim for joy, rather than respectability. Let us make fools of ourselves from time to time, and thus see ourselves, for a moment, as the all-wise God sees us."[130]

Does Mary Play a Role in Opening Our Lives More Fully to the Holy Spirit?

Mary opened her life completely, without the least reserve, to the initiative and action of the Holy Spirit. When she was told that "the Holy Spirit will come upon you, and the power of the Most High will overshadow you" (Luke 1:35), she immediately responded, "Behold, I am the servant of the Lord; let it be to me according to your word" (1:38). At her acceptance, "the Word became flesh" (John 1:14). In this she is the perfect model of surrender. In the Sacred Liturgy, the Church asks God our Father that "through the intercession of the Blessed Mary ever-Virgin our hearts, filled with the light of the Holy Spirit, may constantly strive to cling to Christ, your Son."[131] We can do no better than look to her and ask for her assistance to make our own *fiat*, our own wholehearted yes to the Lord.

As a result of her complete yielding to the Holy Spirit, the Lord was able to do marvelous things through her. When she "entered the house of Zechariah and greeted Elizabeth, . . . the baby leaped in her womb. And Elizabeth was filled with the Holy Spirit, and she exclaimed with a loud cry" (Luke 1:40, 41-42). Guided by the Holy Spirit, she interceded with her Son at the wedding feast in Cana, and as a result, he performed a miracle and many came to believe in him: "This, the first of his signs, Jesus did at Cana in Galilee, and manifested his glory. And his disciples believed in him" (John 2:11).

Through Mary's example and with her help we, too, can become vessels of the Holy Spirit, bringing him into the lives of others. We can also seek her powerful intercession with her Son so that he will reveal his glory and draw souls to himself.

> Like the apostles after Christ's Ascension, the Church must gather in the Upper room "together with Mary, the Mother of Jesus" (Acts 1:4), in order to pray for the Spirit and to gain strength and courage to carry out the missionary mandate. We too, like the apostles, need to be transformed and guided by the Spirit. . . . The whole Church is invited to live more intensely the mystery of Christ by gratefully cooperating in the work of salvation. The Church does this together with Mary and following the example of Mary, the Church's Mother and model.[132]

Pope St. John Paul the Great summarized all of this beautifully:

> Her hands raised, the Virgin Mother of Christ and of the Church prays among us. With her, let us implore and welcome the gift of the Holy Spirit, the light of truth, the power of authentic peace. . . . "Come Holy Spirit, fill the hearts of your faithful, and enkindle in them the fire of your love; though the people spoke different tongues you united them in proclaiming the same faith, alleluia." *Sancte, Spiritus, veni!*[133]

Resources

Resources to help us understand charisms in the life and mission of the Church:
Catechism of the Catholic Church, paragraphs 767–768; 798–801; 951; 2003–2004.

The most dynamic, comprehensive, and accessible workshop on charisms:
The Called and Gifted Workshop, Catherine of Siena Institute, Colorado Springs, CO, https//siena.org.

A thorough, engaging, practical, and ecumenical treatment of the charisms:
Randy Clark and Mary Healy, The Spiritual Gifts Handbook, Chosen Books, 2018.

A theologically rich and penetrating collection of meditations on Pentecost by the Preacher to the Papal Household:
Cardinal Raniero Cantalamessa, The Mystery of Pentecost, Liturgical Press, 2001.

Publications from the CCCB and USCCB:
A CCCB Pastoral Letter: The Charismatic Renewal in Canada, 2003.

Message from the Episcopal Commission for Doctrine of the Canadian Conference of Catholic Bishops for the 50th anniversary of the Charismatic Renewal in Canada, 2018.

A USCCB Pastoral Statement on the Catholic Charismatic Renewal, Bishops' Liaison Committee with the Catholic Charismatic Renewal, 1984.

On the grace of the baptism in the Holy Spirit:

Baptism in the Holy Spirit, The International Catholic Charismatic Renewal Services Doctrinal Commission.

Fr. Francis Martin, *Baptism in the Holy Spirit: Reflections on a Contemporary Grace in the Light of the Catholic Tradition*, St. Bede's Publication, 1998.

Notes

1. Augustine, *On True Religion*, 25.
2. Augustine, *City of God*, 22.8.
3. Possidius, *Life of St. Augustine*, trans. Herbert T. Weiskotten (Princeton University Press, 1919), 19.
4. Pope Paul VI, *The Vital Breath of Grace*, October 10, 1974.
5. Pope Paul VI, *Lumen Gentium*, November 21, 1964, 12, https://www.vatican.va/archive/hist_councils/ii_vatican_council/documents/vat-ii_const_19641121_lumen-gentium_en.html.
6. "Charism" is also applied to ecclesial movements to describe their unique giftedness, spirituality, or mission, but this is not the primary biblical meaning.
7. Randy Clark and Mary Healy, *The Spiritual Gifts Handbook: Using Your Gifts to Build the Kingdom* (Grand Rapids, MI: Chosen Books, 2018), 24.
8. Congregation for the Doctrine of the Faith, *Iuvenescit Ecclesia*, May 15, 2016, 4 https://www.vatican.va/roman_curia/congregations/cfaith/documents/rc_con_cfaith_doc_20160516_iuvenescit-ecclesia_en.html.
9. See Jordan Aumann, *Spiritual Theology* (Evanston, IL: Sheed & Ward Stagbooks, 1980), 422–423.
10. See Jordan Aumann, 422–423.
11. Dr. Mary Healy, "The Church Grows Young: Recent Developments in the Doctrine of Charisms," *Reading and Living Scripture: Essays in Honor of William S. Kurz, SJ*, edited by Jeremy Holmes and Kent J. Lasnoski (Steubenville, OH: Emmaus Academic, 2020).
12. See Jordan Aumann, 422–423. On the biblical evidence that charisms may precede water baptism, see Acts 10 ("The Pentecost of the Gentiles").
13. See Jordan Aumann, 422–423.
14. Cardinal Raniero Cantalamessa, *Come, Creator Spirit: Meditations on the Veni Creator* (Collegeville, MN: Liturgical Press, 2003), 171–181.
15. Jordan Aumann, 422–423.

16. see Jordan Aumann, 208–244.

17. Pope Francis, *Evangelii Gaudium*, November 24, 2013, 259, https://www.vatican.va/content/francesco/en/apost_exhortations/documents/papa-francesco_esortazione-ap_20131124_evangelii-gaudium.html..

18. W. F. Dicharry et al., *New Catholic Encyclopedia*, Encyclopedic Dictionary of the Bible, "Charism: In the Bible," tr. and adap. by l. Hartman (New York, NY: 1963), 350–351.

19. *Iuvenescit Ecclesia*, 6.

20. Irenaeus of Lyon 1994, 2.32.

21. Kilian McDonnell and George T. Montague, "Forum: A Response to Paul Turner on Christian Initiation and Baptism in the Holy Spirit," *Worship*, vol. 71, issue 1 (1997), 51-62.

22. *Iuvenescit Ecclesia*, 4.

23. Cardinal Raniero Cantalamessa proposes that "the place of the charisms was taken over by the 'Seven Gifts of the Spirit' (in Isaiah 11) that, at the beginning and up to Scholasticism, were considered a particular category of charisms promised to the messianic king and later to those who had the task of pastoral governance." In his view, the Seven Gifts are, in fact, a unique category of biblical charisms. "The Catholic Charismatic Renewal: A Current of Grace for the Whole Church," http://www.cantalamessa.org/?p=3760&lang=en.

24. Catherine of Siena Institute, "Frequently Asked Questions about Charisms and Discerning Your Spiritual Gifts," https://siena.org/charisms-faq.

25. St. Catherine of Siena Institute, "What Is the Difference between the Traditional Seven 'Gifts of the Holy Spirit,' Fruits of the Holy Spirit, and Charisms?"

26. Cf. R.J. Tapia, *New Catholic Encyclopedia*, "Charism in the Church," vol. 3, citing Thomas Aquinas, *Summa theologiae* 1a2ae, 111.4.

27. Pope Francis, *Evangelii Gaudium*, 130.

28. As quoted in Congregation for the Doctrine of the Faith, 5.

29. Pope Paul VI, *Lumen Gentium*, 31.

30. Pope John Paul II, Message to the Youth of the World on the Occasion of the IV World Youth Day, August 1989, https://www.vatican.va/content/john-paul-ii/en/messages/youth/documents/hf_jp-ii_mes_27111988_iv-world-youth-day.html.

31. Instruction on Certain Questions Regarding the Collaboration of the Non-Ordained Faithful in the Sacred Ministry of Priest, August 15, 1997, Premise, https://www.vatican.va/roman_curia/pontifical_councils/laity/documents/rc_con_
interdic_doc_15081997_en.html.

32. Instruction on Certain Questions Regarding the Collaboration of the Non-Ordained Faithful in the Sacred Ministry of Priest, Premise.

33. Pope Paul VI, *Apostolicam Actuositatem*, November 18, 1965, 5, https://www.vatican.va/archive/hist_councils/ii_vatican_council/documents/vat-ii_decree_19651118_apostolicam-actuositatem_en.html.

34. Pope Benedict XVI, Message on the Occasion of the Sixth Ordinary Assembly of the International Forum of Catholic Action, August 10, 2012, https://www.vatican.va/content/benedict-xvi/en/messages/pont-messages/2012/documents/hf_ben-xvi_mes_20120810_fiac.html.

35. Pope Paul VI, *Apostolicam Actuositatem*, 3.

36. Pope Francis, *Querida Amazonia*, 94, https://www.vatican.va/content/francesco/en/apost_exhortations/documents/papa-francesco_esortazione-ap_20200202_querida-amazonia.html.

37. Pope Benedict XVI, General Audience, March 28, 2007, https://www.vatican.va/content/benedict-xvi/en/audiences/2007/documents/hf_ben-xvi_aud_20070328.html.

38. St. Irenaeus, *Adversus Haereses*, as summarized in Clement Chinkambako Abenguni Majawa, *The Holy Spirit and Charismatic Renewal in Africa and Beyond (Pneumatological Considerations)* (Catholic University of East Africa, 2007), 69-70.

39. Pope Paul VI, *Apostolicam Actuositatem*, 3.

40. see Pope Paul VI, *Lumen Gentium*, 12.

41. Cardinal Raniero Cantalamessa, "The Catholic Charismatic Renewal: A Current of Grace for the Whole Church," part two, http://www.cantalamessa.org/?p=3760&lang=en.

42. Cardinal Joseph Ratzinger, "The Ecclesial Movements: A Theological Reflection on Their Place in the Church," *Movements in the Church: Proceedings of the World Congress of the Ecclesial Movements* (Vatican City: Pontificium Consilium pro Laicis, 1999), https://www.stucom.nl/document/0058uk1.pdf.

43. *The Pillar*, "The Time for Pentecost Was Fulfilled," May 20, 2021, https://www.pillarcatholic.com/p/the-time-for-pentecost-was-fulfilled.

44. Pope Benedict XVI, Letter to the Bishops of Latin America and the Caribbean, *The Aparecida Document*, http://www.celam.org/aparecida/Ingles.pdf.

45. Quoted in *From Christendom to Apostolic Mission: Pastoral Strategies for an Apostolic Age* (Bismarck, ND: University of Mary, 2020), Preface.

46. Pope John Paul II, *Novo Millennio Ineunte*, January 6, 2001, 40, https://www.vatican.va/content/john-paul-ii/en/apost_letters/2001/documents/hf_jp-ii_apl_20010106_novo-millennio-ineunte.html.

47. Pope Benedict XVI, Letter to the Bishops of the Catholic Church Concerning the Remission of the Excommunication of the Four Bishops Consecrated by Archbishop Lefebvre, March 10, 2009, https://www.vatican.va/content/benedict-xvi/en/letters/2009/documents/hf_ben-xvi_let_20090310_remissione-scomunica.html.

48. Pope Benedict XVI, Letter to the Bishops of the Catholic Church Concerning the Remission of the Excommunication of the Four Bishops Consecrated by Archbishop Lefevre.

49. Pope Francis, *Evangelii Gaudium*, 27.

50. Quoted in *From Christendom to Apostolic Mission: Pastoral Strategies for an Apostolic Age*, preface.

51. Pope Paul VI, *Gaudete in Domino*, May 9, 1975, 7, https://www.vatican.va/content/paul-vi/en/apost_exhortations/documents/hf_p-vi_exh_19750509_gaudete-in-domino.html.

52. Pope John Paul II, *Redemptoris Missio*, December 7, 1990, 40, https://www.vatican.va/content/john-paul-ii/en/encyclicals/documents/hf_jp-ii_enc_07121990_redemptoris-missio.html.

53. Pope Francis, *Evangelii Gaudium*, 259.

54. Pope Francis, Homily, Basilica of Notre-Dame de Quebec, July 28, 2022, https://www.vatican.va/content/francesco/en/homilies/2022/documents/20220728-omelia-vespri-quebec.html.

55. Pope Paul VI, Address to the Participants in the Third International Congress of the Catholic Charismatic Renewal, Rome, May 19, 1975, https://www.vatican.va/content/paul-vi/fr/speeches/1975/documents/hf_p-vi_spe_19750519_rinnovamento-carismatico.html.

56. Pope Paul VI, Address to the Participants in the Third International Congress of the Charismatic Renewal.

57. Pope Paul VI, *Gaudete in Domino*, 7.

58. Pope John Paul II, Audience with Cardinal Suenens and the Council Members of the International Catholic Charismatic Renewal Office, December 11, 1979, https://ingodscompany2.blogspot.com/2013/05/pope-john-paul-ii-affirms-charismatic.html.

59. Pope John Paul II, Address to the Participants of the Sixth International Assembly of the Catholic Charismatic Renewal, May 15, 1987.

60. Pope John Paul II, Address to Leaders of Renewal in the Spirit, April 4, 1998, 1, https://www.vatican.va/content/john-paul-ii/en/speeches/1998/april/documents/hf_jp-ii_spe_19980404_spirito-santo.html.

61. Pope John Paul II, Address to the ICCRO Council, March 12, 1992, 3, https://web.archive.org/web/20070928131946/http:/ccc.garg.com/ccc/articles/John_Paul/John_Paul_001.html.

62. Pope John Paul II, Homily for the Celebration of First Vespers of Pentecost, May 29, 2004, 3, https://www.vatican.va/content/john-paul-ii/en/homilies/2004/documents/hf_jp-ii_hom_20040529_vigil-pentecost.html.

63   Pope John Paul II, Meeting with Ecclesial Movements and New Communities, May 30, 1998.

64. Cardinal Joseph Ratzinger, *The Ratzinger Report* (San Francisco: Ignatius Press, 1985), 44.

65. Cardinal Joseph Ratzinger, *The Ratzinger Report*, 151.

66. Raymond Arroyo, "Interview with Cardinal Ratzinger," *The World Over*, September 5, 2003, https://www.ewtn.com/catholicism/library/world-over-cardinal-ratzinger-interview-2718.

67. Cardinal Joseph Ratzinger, "The Ecclesial Movements: A Theological Reflection on their place in the Church."

68. Pope Benedict XVI, Address to Participants in a Meeting Organized by the Catholic Fraternity of Charismatic Covenant Communities and Fellowships, Oct 31, 2008, https://www.vatican.va/content/benedict-xvi/en/speeches/2008/october/documents/hf_ben-xvi_spe_20081031_carismatici.html.

69   Pope Benedict XVI, Regina Caeli, May 11, 2008.

70. Pope Francis, Address to Participants in the 37th National Convocation of the Renewal in the Holy Spirit, June 1, 2014, https://www.vatican.va/content/francesco/en/speeches/2014/june/documents/papa-francesco_20140601_rinnovamento-spirito-santo.html.

71. Pope Francis, Address to the Renewal in the Holy Spirit Movement, July 3, 2015, https://www.vatican.va/content/francesco/en/speeches/2015/july/documents/papa-francesco_20150703_movimento-rinnovamento-spirito.html.

72. Cardinal Raniero Cantalamessa, "The Catholic Charismatic Renewal: A Current of Grace for the Whole Church." He immediately adds to this statement the following: "I have to add that this is doubly the case for some national churches that for some time have been witnessing a painful hemorrhage of the faithful to other charismatic entities."

73. Pope Paul VI, *Lumen Gentium*, 12.

74. Report of the Sixth Phase of the International Catholic-Pentecostal Dialogue (2011-2015): "Do Not Quench the Spirit:" Charisms in the Life and Mission of the Church, *Cyberjournal for Pentecostal-Charismatic Research*, 13, http://www.pctii.org/cyberj/cyberj24/RomanCatholicPentecostalReport.html.

75. Pope John Paul II, General Audience, August 5, 1998, 3, https://www.vatican.va/content/john-paul-ii/en/audiences/1998/documents/hf_jp-ii_aud_05081998.html.

76. Pope Pius XII, *Mystici Corporis*, June 29, 1943, https://www.vatican.va/content/pius-xii/en/encyclicals/documents/hf_p-xii_enc_29061943_mystici-corporis-christi.html.

77. *Iuvenescit Ecclesia*, 9, cf. *Lumen Gentium*, 4, 7, 11, 12, 25, 30, 50; *Dei Verbum*, 8; *Apostolicam Actuositatem*, 3, 4, 30; *Presbyterorum Ordinis* 4, 9.

78. Pope Paul VI, *Lumen Gentium*, 4.

79. Pope John Paul II, Meeting with Ecclesial Movements and New Communities, May 30, 1998, 4, https://www.vatican.va/content/john-paul-ii/en/speeches/1998/may/documents/hf_jp-ii_spe_19980530_riflessioni.html.

80. Pope John Paul II, General Audience, August 5, 1998, 1.

81. see Pope Paul VI, *Lumen Gentium*, 4.

82. Pope Paul VI, *Lumen Gentium*, 12.

83. Cardinal Raniero Cantalamessa, CHARIS, June 8, 2019, "The Catholic Charismatic Renewal: A Current of Grace for the Whole Church," https://www.charis.international/en/the-catholic-charismatic-renewal-a-current-of-grace-for-the-whole-church/.

84. Eusebius of Caesarea, "Chapter 16: The Circumstances related [to] Montanus and His False Prophets," *Ecclesiastical History*, vol. 5.

85. International Catholic Charismatic Renewal Services Doctrinal Commission, *Baptism in the Holy Spirit* (Locust Grove, VA: National Service Committee of the Catholic Charismatic Renewal in the US, 2012), 56.

86. Weber, Nicholas, *The Catholic Encyclopedia*, vol. 16, "Illuminati," (New York: The Encyclopedia Press, 1914).

87. See Pope Francis, Address to the Renewal in the Holy Spirit Movement.

88. Pope Paul VI, *Evangelii Nuntiandi*, December 8, 1975, 75, https://www.vatican.va/content/paul-vi/en/apost_exhortations/documents/hf_p-vi_exh_19751208_evangelii-nuntiandi.html.

89. Cardinal Joseph Ratzinger, "The Ecclesial Movements: A Theological Reflection on Their Place in the Church."

90. Pope John Paul II, Meeting with Ecclesial Movements and New Communities, 4.

91. *Iuvenescit Ecclesia*, 15.

92. Report of the Sixth Phase of the International Catholic-Pentecostal Dialogue, 11.

93. Pope John Paul II, Meeting with Ecclesial Movements and New Communities, 5.

94. *Iuvenescit Ecclesia*, 15.

95. Pope Francis, Address to Participants in the 37th National Convocation of the Renewal in the Holy Spirit.

96. John Henry Newman, *Sermons Bearing on Subjects of the Day*, (New York: D. Appleton & Co., 1844), 124.

97. *Iuvenescit Ecclesia*, 13.

98. Pope John Paul II, General Audience, August 5, 1998, 2, 5.

99. Cardinal Joseph Ratzinger, "The Ecclesial Movements: A Theological Reflection on Their Place in the Church."

100. See *Iuvenescit Ecclesia*, 10.

101. Pope Benedict XVI, Address to the Members of Communion and Liberation Movement on the 25th Anniversary of Its Pontifical Recognition, March 24, 2007, https://www.vatican.va/content/benedict-xvi/en/speeches/2007/march/documents/hf_ben-xvi_spe_20070324_comunione-liberazione.html.

102. See Pope Francis, Morning Meditation in the Chapel of the *Domus Sanctae Marthae*: God of Surprises, May 8, 2017, https://www.vatican.va/content/francesco/en/cotidie/2017/documents/papa-francesco-cotidie_20170508_god-of-surprises.html.

103. See Rev. Joseph Tixeront, *A Handbook of Patrology* (London: Herder Book Co., 1920), 84–89.

104. Pope John Paul II, General Audience, August 5, 1998, 2.

105. Cardinal Stanislaw Rylko, "The Event of 30 May 1998 and Its Ecclesiological and Pastoral Consequences for the Life of the Church," in *The Ecclesial Movements in the Pastoral Concern of the Bishops* (Vatican City: Pontifical Council of the Laity, 2000), 45.

106. Cardinal Joseph Ratzinger, "The Ecclesial Movements: A Theological Reflection on Their Place in the Church."

107. Pope John Paul II, General Audience, August 5, 1998, 5.

108. Pope Paul VI, *Presbyterorum Ordinis*, December 7, 1965, 6, https://www.vatican.va/archive/hist_councils/ii_vatican_council/documents/vat-ii_decree_19651207_presbyterorum-ordinis_en.html.

109. Pope Paul VI, *Presbyterorum Ordinis*, 9.

110. Pope John Paul II, Address to the Participants in the Fourth International Leaders' Conference of the Catholic Charismatic Renewal, May 7, 1981, 4, https://www.vatican.va/content/john-paul-ii/en/speeches/1981/may/documents/hf_jp-ii_spe_19810507_rinnovamento-carismatico.html.

111. Catherine of Siena Institute, "Frequently Asked Questions about Charisms and Discerning Your Spiritual Gifts: Why Should I Discern My Charisms?" https://siena.org/charisms-faq.

112. Catherine of Siena Institute, "Frequently Asked Questions about Charisms and Discerning Your Spiritual Gifts: How Does Individual Discernment of Charisms Affect the Parish or the Larger Christian Community?"

113. St. Ephrem, cited in Pope John Paul II, *Ecclesia de Eucharistia*, April 17, 2003, 17, https://www.vatican.va/content/john-paul-ii/en/encyclicals/documents/hf_jp-ii_enc_20030417_eccl-de-euch.html.

114. The New Testament does not explicitly describe the baptism of the apostles apart from John's baptism, which was merely a baptism of penance (Acts 19:1-7). However, it must be inferred by the Lord's instruction that it is fundamental to becoming his disciple and on his own command to baptize (John 3:5; Matthew 28:19-20). The apostles themselves insist on the importance of baptism and on its necessity for salvation (Acts 2:38; Acts 22:16; Romans 6:3-4; 2 Corinthians 5:17; Ephesians 5:8; Titus 3:5; 1 Peter 3:21). See also the *Catechism*, 261–263.

115. Pope Benedict XVI, Regina Caeli, May 11, 2008, https://www.vatican. va/content/benedict-xvi/en/angelus/2008/documents/hf_ben-xvi_ reg_20080511_pentecoste.html.

116. Fr. Francis Martin, *Baptism in the Holy Spirit: Reflections on a Contemporary Grace in the Light of the Catholic Tradition* (Petersham, MA: St. Bedes Publications, 1998), 33.

117 St. Thomas Aquinas, *Summa theologiae* (ST) I, q. 43, a. 6.

118. International Catholic Charismatic Renewal Services Doctrinal Commission, *Baptism in the Holy Spirit*, 13.

119. Salvatore Martinez, "Renewal in the Spirit," ZENIT, May 31, 2004, https://www.ewtn.com/catholicism/library/evangelization-and-the-power-of-pentecost-9870..

120. International Catholic Charismatic Renewal Services Doctrinal Commission, *Baptism in the Holy Spirit*, 73.

121. Fr. Bob Bedard, *An Explanation of the Charismatic Renewal*, Companions of the Cross Audio Library, Audio B8, 35:10.

122. Eryn Huntington and Sherry Anne Weddell, *Discerning Charisms* (Seattle: Siena Institute Press, 2000), 12.

123. Salimbene di Adam, in *Monumenta Germaniae*, vol. XXXII, Scriptores, 70, quoted in Randy Clark and Mary Healy, *The Spiritual Gifts Handbook: Using Your Gifts to Build the Kingdom* (Grand Rapids, MI: Baker Publishing Group, 2018).

124. Cardinal Leon-Joseph Suenens, *Renewal and the Powers of Darkness* (Ann Arbor: Servant Books, 1983), x.

125. Pope Benedict XVI, *Deus Caritas Est*, December 25, 2005, 1, https:// www.vatican.va/content/benedict-xvi/en/encyclicals/documents/hf_ben-xvi_enc_20051225_deus-caritas-est.html.

126. Pope Paul VI, *Gaudete in Domino*, Section III.

127. Cardinal Joseph Ratzinger, *Gospel, Catechesis, Catechism: Sidelights on the Catechism of the Catholic Church* (San Francisco: Ignatius Press, 1997), 25.

128. St. Augustine, *The City of God*, XIV.9.

129. St. Thomas Aquinas, *Summa theologiae* I-II, q. 59, a. 5.

130. St. Philip Neri, *Liturgy of the Hours*, Wednesday, Week 8, Ordinary Time.

131. Votive Mass of the Blessed Virgin Mary, Year C: The Holy Name of Mary, Prayer over the Offerings.

132. Pope John Paul II, *Redemptoris Missio*, 92.

133. Pope John Paul II, Homily, May 29, 2004, 5.

Made in the USA
Monee, IL
27 June 2024

60698054R00046